MW00513965

Live Vibrantly!

WITH L.J. & HER DOG
GEORGE ELIOT

L.J. ROHAN
ILLUSTRATIONS BY ALEX MIKEV

For Greg, always the top dog at our house

Introduction

While finishing my return to graduate school—after a thirty-year hiatus—I began thinking about how my new business as a gerontologist would manifest. A friend, and artist, and one of my staunchest supporters and cheerleaders, Ann McIntyre, put forth a novel idea. She suggested adding a visual element to my practice. For the longest time, I couldn't figure out how that would look.

After graduation, my husband and I went on vacation to one of our favorite spots, the mid-coast of Maine. There, relaxing and recharging, I could finally stop and take time to just think. As I walked the beach each day, I asked myself, *how could I incorporate a visual something into a world of words?* Trusting the answer would come at the perfect time, I waited. One afternoon, while stretched out on a blanket, a vision popped into my head. I love clever cartoons; several live under the glass on my desk. I sometimes send particularly funny ones to my friends. Cartoons, cartoons...then my *Aha! moment.* I would include amusing, hand-drawn images on aging to complement my Facebook and website blog posts and other offerings, and share them on all my social media platforms. Adding my precious Havanese puppy, George Eliot, as my sidekick, completed the vision.

The more I thought about this intriguing idea, the more I liked it. Everyone I mentioned it to agreed. Now, how to fill in the details? Since my drawing skills end with stick figures, I needed help to transfer my ideas onto paper. Having worked with a talented young artist, Alex Mikev, on a previous project, I knew he was my man for the job. He said yes, and soon we solidified how George and I would look. We were ready to go!

I draw the rough sketch, add in the dialogue, and Alex works his artistic magic to bring my idea into frame. I find my inspiration all around me—from things I have personally experienced as I am getter older, things my friends say, quotes I read, comments from my readers, and the endless antics of life with George Eliot. I include in this little book a delightful selection of drawings since George and I debuted in January 2018—the day I hung out my sign and opened my door as a gerontologist.

I hope you enjoy my humorous perspectives on aging as much as I enjoy creating them!

Until next time... *Be Vibrant!*

L.J.

Welcome to my life!

*Happiness truly is
a warm puppy!*

All this exercise for my brain wears me out.

Happy Birthday, America!

The many uses of duct tape

George, the Gingerbread Dog

If You Want To Live Vibrantly...

Live like your dog!
(minus the bottom sniffing, stick chewing, and poop eating...)

My Dog's Days of Summer

Counting our blessings...

Music soothes the soul of all creatures

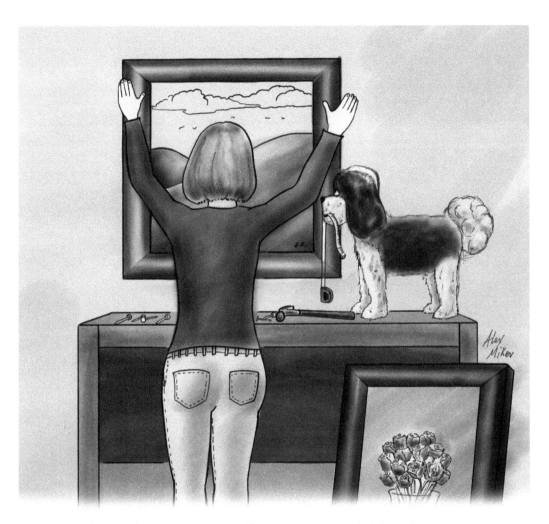

Our desire for beauty around us is timeless.

A wise person said,
"Age does not diminish the extreme disappointment
of having a scoop of ice cream fall from the cone."

We are never too old to have fun and act young.

Acknowledgments

Much of my success, and the realization of this book, I owe to my fabulous team and my wonderful cheerleaders and supporters. Thank you Eric Bradley, Alex Brombal, Nancy Byers, Jacqueline Elizabeth, Gigi Gartner, Maria Jasminoy, Mark Kaufman, Sally Kemp, Craig Kunkel, Aaron Lynn, Ann McIntyre, Charles McMullen, Alex Mikev, Lucie Moebel, Diane Montgomery, Emily Parker, Dylan Robnett, Vicky Wu, my precious muse, George Eliot, and, as always, Greg.

L.J.Rohan, MA, GCG, CAPS

L.J. Rohan is a Gerontologist, author, and speaker, covering the latest scientific research related to aging, the study of gerontology, and Aging-in-Place. She earned a Master's Level Graduate Certification in Gerontology, from the University of Southern California's Davis School of Gerontology. L.J. is also a Certified Aging-in-Place Specialist (CAPS).

L.J. holds undergraduate and graduate degrees from Southern Methodist University. She has been a frequent speaker to groups and at universities, museums, and health-related institutions throughout the United States. L.J. created a Gratitude Meditation[SM] app featuring her hugely popular Gratitude Meditations. The app is available in the iTunes Store and on Google Play. Visit her at LJRohan.com. Follow her on Facebook and Instagram at L.J. Rohan-Gerontologist. L.J. divides her time between Dallas and New York City.

As an illustrator, Alex Mikev visualizes the stories of content experts, filmmakers, and authors using his skills in both traditional and digital artistic media. In collaboration with L.J. Rohan, Mikev illustrates the humor, struggle, and joy that manifests with aging. Informed by his education from Parsons School of Design and Ball State University, he creates artwork for clients as well as in a fine art studio practice. He has exhibited artworks in the Hamiltonian Gallery in Washington D.C., the Indianapolis Arts Center, the Salmagundi Club in New York City, and more. Mikev currently lives and works in Atlanta. His artworks are on view at www.alexmikev.com.